Paul

You're on Your Own, Snoopy

Charles M. Schulz

CORONET BOOKS
Hodder Fawcett, London

Printed and bound in Great Britain for Coronet Books, Hodder Fawcett, London, by Hazell Watson & Viney Ltd, Aylesbury, Bucks

ISBN 0 340 20491 5

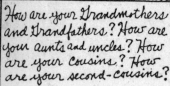

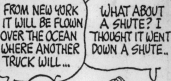

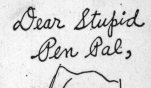

DO YOU THINK IT'S POSSIBLE FOR SOMEONE TO BE IN LOVE AND NOT KNOW IT?

YOU MEAN ME, DON'T YOU?

YOU'RE TALKING ABOUT ME, AREN'T YOU? WHY DON'T YOU COME RIGHT OUT AND SAY IT? WHY DON'T YOU ADMIT IT?

NOW THAT YOU AND I ARE THROUGH, SCHROEDER, WHY DON'T YOU STOP HANGING AROUND MY HOUSE?

THIS ISN'T YOUR HOUSE... THIS IS MY HOUSE!

IT'S AMAZING HOW STUPID YOU CAN BE WHEN YOU'RE IN LOVE..

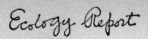

OR WAS I JUDGED ON MY TALENT? IF SO, IS IT RIGHT THAT I BE JUDGED ON A PART OF LIFE OVER WHICH I HAVE NO CONTROL?

IF I WAS JUDGED ON MY EFFORT, THEN I WAS JUDGED UNFAIRLY, FOR I TRIED AS HARD AS I COULD!

WAS I JUDGED ON WHAT I HAD LEARNED ABOUT THIS PROJECT? IF SO, THEN WERE NOT YOU, MY TEACHER, ALSO BEING JUDGED ON YOUR ABILITY TO TRANSMIT YOUR KNOWLEDGE TO ME? ARE YOU WILLING TO SHARE MY "C"?

PERHAPS I WAS BEING JUDGED ON THE QUALITY OF THE COAT HANGER ITSELF OUT OF WHICH MY CREATION WAS MADE...NOW, IS THIS ALSO NOT UNFAIR?

AM I TO BE JUDGED BY THE QUALITY OF COAT HANGERS THAT ARE USED BY THE DRYCLEANING ESTABLISHMENT THAT RETURNS OUR GARMENTS? IS THAT NOT THE RESPONSIBILITY OF MY PARENTS? SHOULD THEY NOT SHARE MY "C"?

"THE SQUEAKY WHEEL GETS THE GREASE!"

flitter
flitter
flitter.

flitter·
flitter
flitter
flutter

flitter
flitter
flutter
flutter
flitter

flitter
flutter
flutter
flitter
flitter
flutter

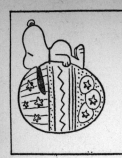

I'VE DECIDED SOMETHING...

IF I EVER GET TO BE A THEOLOGIAN, I'M GOING TO BE WHAT THEY CALL A "THEOLOGIAN IN THE MARKET PLACE"

SO YOU CAN REACH THE PEOPLE?

NO, THAT'S WHERE THE LETTUCE IS!

THIS IS A LETTER TO MISS HELEN SWEETSTORY..

DEAR MISS SWEETSTORY... IT OCCURRED TO ME THAT NO ONE HAS EVER WRITTEN THE STORY OF YOUR LIFE... I SHOULD LIKE TO DO SO...

THEREFORE, I PLAN TO VISIT YOU FOR A FEW WEEKS TO BECOME ACQUAINTED, AND TO GATHER INFORMATION ABOUT YOUR LIFE AND CAREER...

P.S. BEFORE I ARRIVE, PLEASE LOCK UP YOUR CATS!

THERE IT IS! A VINE-COVERED COTTAGE WITH ROSE BUSHES, A WILLOW TREE AND A PICKET FENCE!

THERE IT STANDS, JUST AS I HAD IMAGINED IT! OH, MISS SWEETSTORY, I'VE FOUND YOU AT LAST!

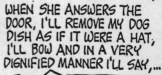

WHEN SHE ANSWERS THE DOOR, I'LL REMOVE MY DOG DISH AS IF IT WERE A HAT, I'LL BOW AND IN A VERY DIGNIFIED MANNER I'LL SAY,...

"HI, SWEETIE!"

A Biography of
Helen Sweetstory

YOU'RE BACK! WHEN DID YOU GET BACK? DID YOU MEET MISS SWEETSTORY? DID YOU INTERVIEW HER? WHAT IS SHE LIKE?

DID SHE ANSWER ALL YOUR QUESTIONS? WAS SHE NICE?

DOES SHE REALLY LIVE IN A VINE-COVERED COTTAGE?

I MAY HAVE TO RENT A STUDIO DOWNTOWN..

Helen Sweetstory was born on a small farm on April 5, 1950.

I THINK I'LL SKIP ALL THE STUFF ABOUT HER PARENTS AND GRANDPARENTS...THAT'S ALWAYS KIND OF BORING...

I'LL ALSO SKIP ALL THE STUFF ABOUT HER STUPID CHILDHOOD... I'LL GO RIGHT TO WHERE THE ACTION BEGAN...

It was raining the night of her high-school prom.

Helen Sweetstory was born on a small farm on April 5, 1950. It was raining the night of her High-School prom.

"LATER THAT SUMMER SHE WAS THROWN FROM A HORSE...A TALL, DARK STRANGER CARRIED HER BACK TO THE STABLES...WAS THIS THE LOVE SHE HAD BEEN SEEKING? TWO YEARS LATER, IN PARIS, SHE..."

IN PARIS?! WHAT ABOUT THE TALL, DARK STRANGER? YOU NEVER GO INTO DETAIL!

WHAT KIND OF A BIOGRAPHER ARE YOU?

I'M A GENTLEMAN BIOGRAPHER!

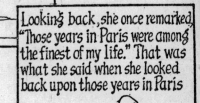

those years in Paris were to be among the finest of her life.

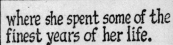

Looking back, she once remarked, "Those years in Paris were among the finest of my life." That was what she said when she looked back upon those years in Paris

where she spent some of the finest years of her life.

I THINK THIS IS GOING TO NEED A LITTLE EDITING...

PSYCHIATRIC HELP 5¢

THE DOCTOR IS IN

I WONDER IF IT'S POSSIBLE REALLY TO MAKE A FRESH START...

PSYCHIATRIC HELP 5¢

THE DOCTOR IS IN

SEE THAT PLANE UP THERE?

IT'S FILLED WITH PEOPLE WHO ARE ALL GOING SOMEPLACE...THAT'S WHAT I'D LIKE TO DO...GO OFF SOMEPLACE, AND START A NEW LIFE...

FORGET IT, CHARLIE BROWN...WHEN YOU GOT OFF THE PLANE, YOU'D STILL BE THE SAME PERSON YOU ARE...

HE DOCTOR

BUT MAYBE WHEN I GOT TO THIS NEW PLACE, THE NEW PEOPLE WOULD LIKE ME BETTER

ONLY UNTIL THEY GOT TO KNOW YOU, CHARLIE BROWN.. THEN YOU'D BE RIGHT BACK WHERE YOU STARTED..

BUT MAYBE THESE NEW PEOPLE WOULD BE MORE UNDERSTANDING

PEOPLE ARE PEOPLE, CHARLIE BROWN...

WELL, MAYBE I..

FORGET IT, CHARLIE BROWN

BUT..

NOPE!

UH..

FIVE CENTS, PLEASE

SIGH

ONCE YOU HAVE A PATIENT HOOKED, LAND HIM!

WHAT'S THIS ABOUT OUR FAVORITE SPORT?

THE LATEST POLL SHOWS THAT FOOTBALL IS FAVORED BY 36% OF THE FANS, BASEBALL 21%, BASKETBALL 8%, BOWLING 4%, HOCKEY 3% AND SO ON...

WELL?

WELL, WHAT?

WELL, WHAT ABOUT KISSING AND HUGGING?!

WE'RE GOING TO HAVE TO LEARN THE METRIC SYSTEM, FRANKLIN..

BY THE TIME WE GROW UP, THE METRIC SYSTEM WILL PROBABLY BE OFFICIAL..

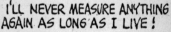

ONE INCH IS 2.54 CENTIMETERS.. ONE FOOT IS 0.3048 METERS AND ONE MILE IS 1.609 KILOMETERS...

I'LL NEVER MEASURE ANYTHING AGAIN AS LONG AS I LIVE!

IF THE SUN IS SHINING, YOU CAN RIDE AROUND IN YOUR CONVERTIBLE AND BE HAPPY... IF IT STARTS TO RAIN, IT WON'T SPOIL YOUR DAY BECAUSE YOU CAN JUST SAY, "OH, WELL, THE RAIN WILL FILL UP MY LAKE!"

WHAT DO YOU THINK THE SECRET OF LIVING IS, SNOOPY?

SMAK!

A CONVERTIBLE AND A LAKE.. I DON'T KNOW ABOUT YOU, CHUCK...

IF YOUR LAKE IS DRYING UP, YOU CAN SAY, "OH, WELL, THIS IS NICE WEATHER FOR RIDING IN A CONVERTIBLE.."

THERE I WAS..RESTING COMFORTABLY...

SUDDENLY I WAS PLAGUED BY A SELF-DOUBT!

DO MY EYES DECEIVE ME? ARE YOU GOING TO BED WITHOUT YOUR SECURITY BLANKET?

I GAVE IT TO SNOOPY TO HOLD FOR ME...I'M GOING TO BREAK THE HABIT THIS TIME IF IT KILLS ME..I TOLD HIM NOT TO GIVE IT BACK NO MATTER HOW MUCH I BEG...

I WOULDN'T TRUST THAT STUPID BEAGLE WITH ANYTHING!

WHY NOT? I'M SURE HE'S PUT IT AWAY IN VERY SAFE KEEPING...

I HAVEN'T SLEPT FOR TWO DAYS! I WANT MY BLANKET BACK!

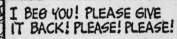

THIS IS WHY I TOLD YOU TO KEEP IT FOR ME... I THOUGHT I COULD GIVE IT UP, BUT I CAN'T.. I'VE GOT TO HAVE IT BACK!

I BEG YOU! PLEASE GIVE IT BACK! PLEASE! PLEASE!

THIS IS FUN!

PSYCHIATRIC HELP 5¢

THE DOCTOR IS [IN]

SO I BOUGHT LINUS A NEW BLANKET... I THOUGHT I WAS DOING THE RIGHT THING..

HMM... I'M NOT QUITE SURE HOW I CAN PUT THIS, CHARLIE BROWN, BUT LET ME SAY THIS...

IN ALL OF MANKIND'S HISTORY, THERE HAS NEVER BEEN MORE DAMAGE DONE THAN BY PEOPLE WHO "THOUGHT THEY WERE DOING THE RIGHT THING"

FIVE CENTS, PLEASE!

SIGH

THE DOCTOR IS [IN]

⟹

I THINK IT STARTED BECAUSE OF SOMETHING THAT HAPPENED AT A PLAYGROUND... I WAS PLAYING IN A SANDBOX WITH A COUPLE OF OTHER KIDS...I CAN'T EVEN REMEMBER WHO THEY WERE...

ANYWAY, ALL OF A SUDDEN, ONE OF THEM POURED A WHOLE BUCKET OF SAND OVER MY HEAD...I STARTED CRYING, I GUESS, AND MY MOTHER CAME RUNNING UP, AND TOOK ME HOME

IT'S KIND OF EMBARRASSING NOW TO TALK ABOUT IT

ANYWAY, THE NEXT DAY WE DROVE OUT TO THE DAISY HILL PUPPY FARM, AND MY MOTHER AND DAD BOUGHT ME A DOG...

GOOD GRIEF!

IT'S A MISTAKE TO TRY TO AVOID THE UNPLEASANT THINGS IN LIFE..

POW!

BUT I'M BEGINNING TO CONSIDER IT...

CHOMP
CHOMP
CHOMP

MAYBE I CAN GET AN
ADVANCE ON TOMORROW
NIGHT'S DINNER..

RATS..I'M
STILL
HUNGRY..

ANOTHER
ADVANCE?

I HAVE A SUGGESTION TO MAKE.

I SUGGEST THAT THE BOARD OF EDUCATION BE TOLD TO BUY A HERD OF TWENTY-FOUR HORSES...

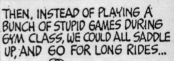

THEN, INSTEAD OF PLAYING A BUNCH OF STUPID GAMES DURING GYM CLASS, WE COULD ALL SADDLE UP, AND GO FOR LONG RIDES...

LOTS OF GOOD SUGGESTIONS NEVER GET OFF THE GROUND!

TAKE THAT, YOU STUPID SCHOOL!!

BOOT!

I LIKE SUMMER VACATION... IT'S THE ONLY TIME WHEN YOU CAN RUN RIGHT UP TO A SCHOOL AND KICK IT!

"IN THE BOOK OF LIFE, THE ANSWERS ARE NOT IN THE BACK!"

THAT'S MY NEW PHILOSOPHY

I THINK YOU'RE IN TROUBLE

ANOTHER GOOD ONE IS, "SHOW 'IM THE HIGH, HARD ONE!"

COULD YOU WRITE SOME OF THOSE DOWN? I'LL NEVER BE ABLE TO REMEMBER THEM OTHERWISE

THANK YOU... THIS WILL BE A BIG HELP..

"OKAY, PITCHER, THROW IT PAST HIM! HE CAN'T HIT WHAT HE CAN'T SEE!"

"PITCH HARD, CHARLIE BROWN!"

"STAY WITH 'IM, KID! YOU CAN DO IT, CHARLIE BROWN! BE GOOD, BOY! GOOD SHOT! SHOW 'IM THE HIGH, HARD ONE.."

⋇ SIGH ⋇

SHE DID IT! SHE HIT A HOME RUN!

AND, YOU'RE GOING TO HAVE TO STAND OUT BY HOME PLATE, AND KISS HER! YOU PROMISED!!

SHE'S ROUNDING FIRST...SHE'S ROUNDING SECOND..SHE'S ROUNDING THIRD..SHE'S HEADING FOR HOME! IT'S KISSING TIME! LA DE DA DE DA DE DA DE DA

I APPRECIATE YOUR TAKING ME ALONG TO PLAY TENNIS, LINUS...

..THAT'S THE ONLY TROUBLE WITH TENNIS.. YOU CAN'T PLAY IT ALONE

MAYBE WE WON'T GET TO PLAY AT ALL... THE COURTS ARE ALL FULL..

THE COURTS ARE ALWAYS FULL WITH BIG KIDS, AND THEY NEVER LET YOU PLAY... I HATE BIG KIDS! THEY NEVER GIVE YOU A CHANCE!

THEY'LL PLAY ALL DAY...JUST YOU WATCH! THEY'LL HOG THE COURTS ALL DAY! THEY'LL NEVER QUIT...THEY'LL JUST KEEP ON PLAYING AND PLAYING, AND THEY'LL NEVER...

YOU BIG KIDS GET OFF THAT COURT RIGHT NOW, OR MY BOY FRIEND WILL CLOBBER YOU!!

THAT'S THE ONLY TROUBLE WITH TENNIS... YOU CAN'T PLAY IT ALONE

GOOD GRIEF, ANOTHER RAINY DAY...THIS IS THE DORKIEST WEATHER I'VE EVER SEEN!

YOU SHOULDN'T CRITICIZE THE WEATHER, SIR...IT'S ALL PART OF THE WORLD WE LIVE IN...

STOP CALLING ME "SIR"

BESIDES, THIS RAIN IS PROBABLY HELPING SOME FARMER, WHICH, OF COURSE, BRINGS UP ANOTHER POINT...

I'VE NEVER SEEN A FARMER GO TO SUMMER CAMP, HAVE YOU, SIR?

I CAN'T STAND IT!

SCHULZ

AH, ANOTHER LETTER FROM WOODSTOCK WHO'S AT EAGLE CAMP.

" DEAR FRIEND OF FRIENDS... TODAY WE HEARD A SPECIAL LECTURE BY A CATERPILLAR WHO HAD CRAWLED ALL THE WAY ACROSS A FREEWAY WITHOUT GETTING RUN OVER.. "

" IT WAS A VERY EXCITING ADVENTURE...HE HAD ALL OF US SITTING ON THE EDGE OF OUR BRANCHES! HA HA "

THAT WOODSTOCK!

SIR, I'M SORRY I WOKE YOU UP LAST NIGHT

STOP CALLING ME "SIR," AND FORGET ABOUT LAST NIGHT..THAT'S WHAT TENT MONITORS ARE FOR..

MY STOMACH FEELS BETTER TODAY.. THIS IS A NICE CAMP, BUT I THINK IT WOULD BE BETTER IF THERE WERE SOME BOYS...

THE BOYS' CAMP IS ACROSS THE LAKE...I KNOW A COUPLE OF PRETTY NEAT BOYS WHO ARE THERE, TOO...

HOW ABOUT YOU AND I SCAMPERING AROUND THE LAKE TONIGHT ON OUR LITTLE MAMA CASS LEGS AND VISITING THEM?

"MAMA CASS LEGS"?

AH, ANOTHER LETTER FROM WOODSTOCK!

"DEAR FRIEND OF FRIENDS... I AM A FAILURE... I HAVE JUST WASHED OUT OF EAGLE CAMP... I FEEL TERRIBLE..."

"I HAD ALWAYS DREAMED OF SOMEDAY BEING AN EAGLE AND SOARING HIGH ABOVE THE CLOUDS, BUT NOW MY DREAMS ARE OVER... I WAS WASHED OUT FOR GETTING TOO MANY BEAK-BLEEDS.."

POOR WOODSTOCK!

SCHULZ

CHUCK! WE'RE HERE! I TOLD YOU WE'D COME, AND WE DID!

WE GOT LONELY SO WE SCAMPERED AROUND THE POND ON OUR LITTLE RUBY KEELER LEGS, AND HERE WE ARE! I'LL BET YOU'RE GLAD TO SEE ME, HUH, CHUCK?

WHERE'S SNOOPY? NOW, THAT'S A FINE THING..I WAS GONNA FIX HIM UP WITH MY DORKY LITTLE FRIEND HERE, AND NOW HE'S RUN OFF..

HOW ABOUT **THIS** KID, CHUCK? IS HE A FRIEND OF YOURS? INTRODUCE US, HUH, CHUCK?

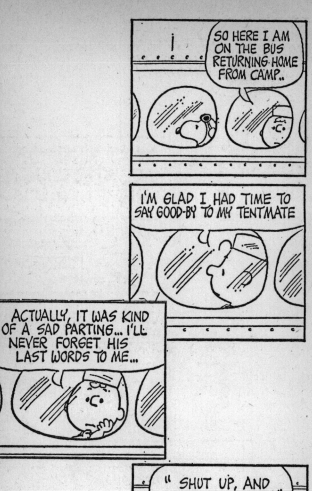

IS LOVE A 'NOW' KIND OF THING, CHUCK, OR IS IT MOSTLY HOPE AND MEMORIES?

WELL, MY DAD SAYS THAT HE TOOK A GIRL TO THE MOVIES ONCE, AND IT WAS ONE OF THOSE REAL SAD LOVE STORIES...

HE REMEMBERED THAT ANNE BAXTER WAS IN IT, AND FOR YEARS AFTERWARD, EVERY TIME HE SAW ANNE BAXTER, HE'D GET REAL DEPRESSED BECAUSE IT WOULD REMIND HIM OF THAT MOVIE AND THE GIRL HE HAD BEEN WITH...

HE NEVER FORGOT THAT GIRL BECAUSE EVERY TIME HE SAW ANNE BAXTER, IT WOULD REMIND HIM OF HER...

THEN, ONE NIGHT ON THE LATE, LATE SHOW, THAT SAME MOVIE CAME ON, BUT IT TURNED OUT THAT HE HAD BEEN WRONG ALL THOSE YEARS... IT WASN'T ANNE BAXTER... IT WAS SUSAN HAYWARD!

LOVE HAS ITS MEMORIES, I GUESS

I WAS REALLY HOPING IT WAS A 'NOW' KIND OF THING

IT IS FOR SOME OF US, SWEETIE!

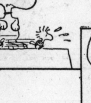

THE LATEST PEANUTS

All these books are available at your local bookshop or newsagent, or can be ordered direct from the publisher. Just tick the titles you want and fill in the form below.

Prices and availability subject to change without notice.

....

CORONET BOOKS, P.O. Box 11, Falmouth, Cornwall.

Please send cheque or postal order, and allow the following for postage and packing:

U.K.—One book 18p plus 8p per copy for each additional book ordered, up to a maximum of 66p.

B.F.P.O. and EIRE—18p for the first book plus 8p per copy for the next 6 books, thereafter 3p per book.

OTHER OVERSEAS CUSTOMERS—20p for the first book and 10p per copy for each additional book.

Name...

Address...

....